MW0117387

CONTENTS

THE BLESSING:

Keys to the Kingdom:
ACCESS GRANTED
By Eric Williams

ERIC T. WILLIAMS

FORWARD

It is with great joy and anticipation that introduce to you "THE BLESS: Keys To The Kingdom: Access Granted" by Eric T. Williams. This book embodies five words that perfectly capture its essence: essential, profound, revealing, reflective, and God-centered.

Having had the privilege of knowing Eric for the past ten years, I can attest to the depth of insight and spiritual maturity he brings to the body of Christ. He is a true voice sent to guide believers away from traditional religious mindsets towards a deeper understanding and experience of Kingdom reality.

In a world where the concept of blessing is often misunderstood and misinterpreted, Eric's book sheds light on the true nature of God's blessings. Too often, we prioritize material possessions and outward signs of success as indicators of God's favor, neglecting the deeper spiritual blessings that flow from alignment with His will.

Within the Kingdom of God, blessings are not defined by worldly standards but by divine origin and alignment with God's will. Eric's work reveals key principles that unlock the fullness of God's blessings and positions the reader to receive and walk in all that God has ordained.

I pray this book helps you realize the treasures of God's blessings and align your life with his divine purpose. I'm confident you'll be enriched, inspired and transformed as you embark on this journey of discovery with Eric as your faithful guide.

May you receive all that the Father intends to impart to you through this anointed work.

Braden E. Friday
Senior Pastor of Living Water Ministries Incorporated Lynn Haven Florida and
a Lead Pastor with Pastors United Bay County Florida

CHAPTER 1: THE FATHER'S BLESSING: PART 1

As a loving parent cradles a newborn child, there is a profound moment where the fullness of love, a commitment that defies articulation, envelops the helpless infant. You, beloved, are that child in the arms of the Almighty Father. With an unwavering promise, He pours out His love to you—love that provides, protects, empowers, equips, and blesses beyond measure. From the dawn of creation, the Father has intricately woven His essence into your being, imprinting you with His divine DNA, marking you with His abundant grace.

Think upon Adam, sculpted from the earth, yet a full-grown babe in spirit, cradled in an Eden prepared with care, a garden abundant and fruitful. Just as a father today would adorn a nursery with tokens of love and joy, our Heavenly Father appointed every tree, stream, and creature as gifts for his cherished child's delight. Adam opened his eyes not just to a new world, but to a legacy—as the bearer of God's own image and likeness. He was the epitome of the Father's intricate design, the only creation endowed with the power to mirror the divine.

In you, this legacy endures. Each breath you draw is a testament to His enduring blessing, a reminder that in His eyes, you are precious and purposeful. Let this assurance settle in your heart as the sunrise heralds a new day: you are infinitely valued, thoroughly known, and relentlessly loved by the Father. As you step into the light of this truth, you will find strength, solace, and the courage to grow into the fullness of the divine purpose sewn into your very fabric.

Divine inheritance – isn't that a phrase that is worthy of meditating on? It's like finding out you had a rich uncle who left you a sprawling estate in Tuscany... but so, so much more. This inheritance isn't about earthly acres or vintage wines; it's about something eternal and priceless that's been lovingly tucked into our spiritual DNA by the Creator Himself.

You see, just the other day, as I was attempting to meditate (and mostly succeeding in listing groceries in my head), I had a realization. We're a bit like old-fashioned radios, built with the capacity to tune into God's frequency - some call it divine whisper or still small voice. But often, we're too busy scanning through static to hear the music of His guidance.

This divine inheritance is not just a promise—it's a potential, a capacity wired within us to connect, to create, to cultivate goodness in the likeness of our Heavenly Father. Like a trust fund that matures over time, this legacy unfolds within us, growing richer as we dare to align our hearts to His purpose.

Here's the funny part though, as much as we have access to this heavenly treasury, we tend to stumble over our own feet in pursuit of pennies, neglecting the gold mines within us. It's like choosing those stale cheese crackers in your pantry over a chef's five-course dinner.

So, let's not forget the divine inheritance ticket that's sitting right in our back pocket. It's not just about claiming it but also about using it; investing it in acts of kindness, painting the world with the vibrant colors of love and compassion, and sculpting moments with patience and gratitude. Now that's an inheritance worth living for, and certainly worth passing on!

CHAPTER 2: THE FATHER'S BLESSING: PART 2

The Blessing. Consider it the driver's license to our divine inheritance, the apropos ID card that says, "Yes, you may indeed take this beauty out for a spin." And here's a little something to chew on—imagine being perched on the cusp of adolescence, eyes wide with all the earnestness of a pup. There in the driveway sits a shiny car; dad pats it and says, "All yours, kiddo—when the time's right."

Flash forward a smidge, and there you are, a preteen with dreams as big as dad's car keys. You're polishing the hood, you're sitting in the driver's seat, making vroom-vroom noises, maybe even fussing with the rearview mirror. It's yours, the inheritance is solid, but... the keys aren't yet in hand. You lack the blessing—the nod that says, "Go ahead, take it for a real drive."

Now, bear with me—just as you're about to set foot into teendom, the DMV is your new best friend. That permit, that glorious testament to your growing-upness, arrives. You slide into the driver's seat, not just to pretend, but to truly steer where you wish to go. That, my friends, is joy unspeakable.

So why is it, then, that we, as Christians, as earnest followers of the Way, sometimes sit on our hands, thumbing through the inheritance manual without ever firing up the engine? Eden was Adam's inheritance—lush, limitless, and his for the tending. But as the story goes, a slip, a snag in his spiritual paperwork, and poof —there went the keys.

And it's here that the plot thickens. The Blessing—it isn't just a pat on the back or a kindly nod. It's the divine power of attorney, the "legal" spiritual document, reinstated by none other than Christ Himself. It's the heavenly stamp in your passport, the "operational permit" that re-opens the gates of Eden's model of living, a return to our intended state, where sonship and stewardship walk hand in hand, as we tend to our inheritance with the love and audacity of true heirs. To live that blessed life—and to think, all along, the keys were ours to claim.

Remember, as believers, we have been given the ultimate inheritance through Christ's sacrifice on the cross. We have access to a life of abundance and purpose, filled with joy and love beyond measure. Yet, sometimes we forget that the keys to this inheritance are already in our hands.

Just like a teenager receiving their driver's permit, we too must take hold of our spiritual inheritance and actively use it to navigate through life. We cannot simply sit back and read about it, we must put it into action.

But just like Adam in the garden of Eden, there may be obstacles that make us feel as if we have lost our inheritance or can no longer access its full potential. Thankfully, through Jesus Christ, our divine power of attorney has been reinstated and our inheritance has been fully restored.

Let us always remain conscious of the power that resides within us through Christ. We are called to walk boldly as true heirs, tending to our inheritance with love and audacity. And let us never forget that the keys to this abundant life have always been ours for the taking. Our only task is to believe, yield, and walk it out. The claiming of our inheritance is eternally coupled with confidence of Christ and joy of Spirit.

As we tie the ribbons on these first thoughts, it's fitting to rest for a moment in the hush of gratitude and laugh at the memory of our shared stumbles and the lessons they've unfurled. By grace, indeed, we stand - marveling at the golden thread woven through the cloth of our days, small miracles wrapped up in the ordinary.

"Count your blessings," they say, and perhaps they're onto something—the blessedness isn't merely in the counting, but in awakening to the reality that we are the counted. Each of us, a treasured note in the symphony of creation, echoing our Maker's heartbeat. In my own journey, there've been times when I've felt more like a discordant clang than a harmonious chord, but even the clangs find their place in the score, don't they?

Remember this, that in the laughter of a child or the hush of a sunrise, you're witnessing the echoes of heavenly blessings. Look closely, and you'll see them, even in the midst of the vicissitudes of life —at your feet, in your hands, over your head. We are blessed, not because of our striving or worthiness, but simply because we are extravagantly loved, held in the arms of grace that neither slumber nor sleep.

CHAPTER 3: ACCESS GRANTED - THE EXCLUSIVE KEY TO KINGDOM

One day, I found myself in need of retrieving a file safely stored away in a secure lockbox. With anticipation, I attempted to unlock it using various keys, none of them seemed to fit. But then I remembered the key hole was actually a façade, that could be moved in order to reveal an hi-tech finger scan. I had tried every key that I possessed, forgetting that this lockbox was uniquely design to unlock with my identity verification, my thumb print. And only one of my fingers could be used, my right thumb held the power to grant entry. You see, it was my right thumb that I had programmed into the thumb recognition security system. Finally, I remembered, and as I scanned my right thumb, I heard a satisfying click—the box was unlocked. It became clear that only my right thumb possessed the qualification to unlock the lockbox.

Similarly, in Leviticus chapter 8, we read about the consecration of Aaron's sons, the priests. In the ceremony, their right ear, right thumb, and right foot were anointed with blood and oil. God's specificity regarding the finger to anoint draws attention to an important principle.

In the same way, accessing anything pertaining to the kingdom of God requires specificity—a divine qualification that cannot be obtained through man's philosophy, religion, denominationalism, or personal efforts. No matter what means we attempt to use, the only acceptable key to access the kingdom is Christ Jesus.

For far too long, religion has attempted to force open the kingdom using its own practices and traditions, only to be met with the resounding answer: access denied. Even in the days of Jesus, the religious leaders claimed to be the exclusive gatekeepers to access God. No longer do we require a priest or prophet as our mediator. In fact, John the Baptist was the last mediator between God and man. The law and the prophets all pointed to him, but now, it is Jesus alone who stands as the mediator.

The religious systems of old could no longer hold the title of gatekeepers to the kingdom. Jesus dismantled the barriers that limited access, offering a new and direct way to the Father. He became the key that unlocks the doors of the kingdom, offering open access to all who believe in him.

Religion, throughout history, has attempted to proclaim various paths to access the kingdom of God. However, these paths have always fallen short, leaving seekers wandering in a maze of confusion. But the truth is, access to the kingdom can never be achieved through our own efforts or the empty promises of human wisdom.

In a world that offers countless philosophies and religions, it is easy to get lost in the noise. Many claim to have the key to accessing the divine, but in reality, they are mere imitations that cannot unlock the true treasures of the kingdom. It is only in Christ that we find the exclusive blessing that grants us access to the boundless riches of the kingdom.

Christ Jesus is the embodiment of divine love and wisdom. He came to fulfill the law and the prophets, to bridge the gap between humanity and God, and to offer a path of salvation and eternal life. His life, death, and resurrection stand as the ultimate testimony to his exclusive role in granting access to the kingdom.

As we ponder the blessing, we must grasp its profound nature—it is not a mere gift or token of favor. The blessing transcends such simplicity, for it emerges from the glorious outpouring of the Father, the ultimate Source of all things. All glory emanates from Him, and the Son shines forth as the manifest Glory of the Father. It is through the Son that the blessing flows, like a majestic river of divine abundance.

It is crucial to recognize that the blessing is intricately linked to the identity of Christ. He freely imparts this divine identity to those who place their faith in him. This identification is not superficial but deeply transformative. Through his perfect sacrifice on the cross, his glorious identity becomes accessible to all who believe.

The blessing, flowing from the Son, is entrusted to the sons of God —those who are led by the Spirit of God. This union of the divine blessing with human vessels ushers forth true worship and praise unto the Father. The sons of God, as recipients and custodians of the blessing, enter into a sacred partnership with Christ. They reflect his glory, revealing his character, and magnifying the love of the Father.

To flow in the blessing means to operate in that which brings forth glory for the Father. It is not a selfish endeavor, but rather a conduit for the divine. As we surrender to the guidance of the Spirit, the blessing manifests through us, impacting the world around us. Through us, the blessing becomes a tangible expression of the Father's love and grace.

In essence, the blessing is not separate from the identity of Christ —it is an integral part of it. Through his sacrifice on the cross, we are united with him, sharing in the same divine identity. The blessing becomes our birthright, a testament to the redemptive power of Christ, and a reminder of the immense love the Father has bestowed upon us.

The blessing is intricately connected to the identity of Christ, emanating from the Father and flowing through the Son. It is through our faith in him, and his perfect sacrifice, that this transcendent blessing becomes available to us. Let us embrace the divine identity imparted to us and flow in the blessing, magnifying the glory of the Father and reflecting the love of Christ to the world.

The blessing that Christ possesses is unparalleled in its depth and significance. It encompasses the forgiveness of sins, reconciliation with God, restoration of brokenness, and the promise of eternal life. It offers a way out of darkness and into the glorious light of the kingdom. Such a blessing cannot be found elsewhere, for it is exclusive to Christ alone.

Religious practices, human achievements, or self-effort can never attain the blessing that only Christ can give. The keys to the kingdom are held securely within his grasp, and he willingly extends them to all who surrender their lives to him. It is through him that we gain access to divine wisdom, guidance, and the transformative power to live a life that aligns with the kingdom's values.

Jesus himself declared, "I am the door. If anyone enters by Me, he will be saved and will go in and out and find pasture." These words resonate with the truth of his exclusivity as the key to accessing the boundless provisions and promises of the kingdom.

Never forget this truth, the exclusive key to access the kingdom of God is Christ Jesus. No religious practice, tradition, or personal effort can gain us entry. Jesus boldly declared himself as the only way to the Father. He is the mediator, the doorway to intimate communion with the divine. Let us abandon our reliance on man-made systems and embrace the truth that in Jesus, we find the ultimate access granted to the kingdom.

CHAPTER 4. THE FINISHED WORK OF CHRIST: THE GATEWAY TO LASTING BLESSINGS

You know, there's something quite astonishing about the finished work of Christ—it's a bit like finding an old, dusty lamp in Grandma's attic, only to discover it's an antique of immeasurable value. This profound undertaking, Christ's sacrifice and victory, may seem like historical footnotes to some, barely flickering in the vastness of our bustling lives. Yet to those with eyes to see, it is the lighthouse guiding weary travelers home, the all-access pass into a realm where we're not just scraping by, but truly flourishing.

In my own walk, I used to imagine that I could contribute to this work, as if it was an ongoing construction site and I was a tradesman arriving with my well-worn toolbox. But, as I've come to realize, the work is complete. The power of this revelation hits differently, like the gentle yet undeniable splash of a baptismal pool. It's there, in the simplicity of just "being" rather than "doing," that we find a wellspring of blessings so pure, so potent, that they transform the very fabric of our existence.

And isn't it a bit funny? We scurry around searching for keys to treasures untold, forgetting that the door has always stood ajar, the feast waiting with our place at the table lovingly set. So laugh with me, friends, at our collective forgetfulness, and let's step through that portal once more, basking in the warmth of the ultimate gift, for in Christ, we have not just a trickle of goodness, but an endless cascade of blessings just waiting to be claimed. We must claim them, my friend, and keep on claiming them as we continue to journey towards our ultimate destination.

In the end, it all comes down to faith. Believing in the unseen, holding onto hope when everything else seems to crumble. Faith is not just a belief system or a set of rules; it is an active trust in something greater than ourselves. It is a choice we make every day, even when the world around us may try to shake that foundation. But as we continue on this faith journey, let's remember to be gentle with ourselves and others, for it is not an easy path to walk.

Biblical faith is like holding onto the sun's rays - a hopeful assurance in what we cannot see but somehow know to be truer than the ground beneath our feet. It's not blind optimism; it's a deeply rooted certainty that there's a master plan, an artist behind the canvas of our lives, mixing shades and colors we might not understand just yet.

I remember January 2019, as if it was yesterday, a time when the sky seemed to fall on me. My brother Nate, my mom, my grandmother, and my cousin due to unrelated circumstances lost their lives, I felt like Job. The pain was unimaginable, the kind that gnaws at your soul, leaving you gasping for air, wondering if the sun will ever rise again. In the thick of my grief, the Father whispered a promise, like a lifeline thrown into stormy seas – "For I know the plans I have for you," declares the Lord, "plans to prosper you and not to harm you, plans to give you hope and a future" (*Jeremiah 29:11*).

In that heart-shattering moment, I found something to "Faith On To." Not a simple resolution to my sorrows, but a sacred assurance that beyond the veil of my despair, a dawn was coming. So, I clung to that promise, each word a stepping stone leading out of the valley of the shadows of death. And as I journeyed through each day, the Father's faithfulness became the curtain on which my healing was woven – thread by thread, a testament to Love's unyielding grasp.

As we navigate through our own faith journeys, let us not forget that we are all imperfect beings, prone to doubt and mistakes. It is in these moments of imperfection that we can find the greatest growth and understanding. The struggles and challenges we face do not define us, but rather nudges us into experiential reality of who we actually are.

How often we find ourselves in the belly of the whale, much like Jonah – confined, disoriented and in the dark about what comes next. But even inside the belly of that great fish, our Father is at work. Reflect on the verse from **Jonah 2:2**: "In my distress I called to the Lord, and he answered me. From deep in the realm of the dead I called for help, and you listened to my cry." It's a reminder of how our cries aren't simply echoes in the abyss but are heard and answered by a Father who specializes in impossible rescues.

Whenever I find myself grasping for control, feeling swallowed by the circumstances, I smile at Jonah's predicament and think to myself, "If God can steer a whale, surely He can navigate me through this." Just like Jonah, we may be spit out on new shores, baffled but better equipped for the journey ahead, our faith deepened, not in spite of the whale ride, but because of it. So, the next time you feel like you've been digested whole by life's trials, remember Jonah. That situation just might be your transportation to where you need to be—thrown not with disregard, but purposeful aim, by the hands of the Divine Navigator.

Just as I find comfort in Jonah's aquatic detour, I revel in pondering the divine engineering of our own misadventures. Isn't it a hoot to think that our dilemmas, those seemingly insurmountable obstacles, are all part of a master plan? They're there, you see, not as stumbling blocks but as stepping stones, reminding us of who we are as a result of Christ's finished work. And let me tell you, there's no better feeling than being regurgitated, metaphorically speaking, onto life's shore after a tumultuous season. Even in the mess—fish vomit and all—I bet Jonah was planting smooches on that sandy beach like there was no tomorrow.

And when we see our troubles as gateways to blessings, a joy unspeakable floods our souls. "For as Jonah was three days in the belly of the whale, so will the Son of Man be three days in the heart of the earth" (Matthew 12:40). What a beautiful truth! Just as Jonah was unceremoniously ejected onto shore, we find ourselves, through our union with Christ and our baptism into His death, catapulted into the resurrection's splendor. Now, as He is, so are we—in the here and now—spit up by grace and poised on the precipice of our God-given destiny. Our resurrected life, though, isn't a cumbersome thing we lug around; it's as light as a feather because it is by faith that we find ourselves seated with Christ in the heavenly realms. What a blessing, indeed!

Isn't it amazing to think that our troubles are not just random events, but part of a grand plan designed by the hand of our Loving Father? Even when we feel lost at sea like Jonah, we can trust that there is purpose and meaning behind every storm. And just like Jonah was ultimately rescued and brought to shore, we too can find hope and joy in the midst of our trials, knowing that they are ultimately for our good and God's glory.

Oh, the tangled webs we weave. Jonah, with feet planted firmly in the wrong direction; Adam, plucking forbidden fruit in defiance; and us—yes, us—collecting our own medley of choices, each one seasoned with a dash of rebellion. It's a family tradition, it seems, passed down through generations like that one dubious casserole recipe nobody really likes. But enter stage right: Jesus. The pivot in this plot, the twist in the tale. He showed up, took a deep, heavenly breath, and chose—oh, think of it!—to step firmly into the mess of humanity in full obedience to the Father.

In his extraordinary 'yes' to the Father, Christ flung wide open the gates of blessing, creating an everlasting stream where our access is not granted by lofty deeds or cautious tiptoeing around the tightropes of morality. My friend, this is the masterpiece of Jesus' finished work. He did not simply walk the tightrope for us; he actually utilized the tightrope (the Law), fulfilling it on our behalf and constructing a bridge that connects the heavenly and the earthly, thus bridging the gap in our estranged relationship with the Father. His redemptive act effectively eliminated the ravine between us and the kingdom of God. So now, instead of getting ensnared in the sticky webs of our own creation, we can dance (or shuffle, depending on your rhythm) into a life marked by His completed work. And that, my friends, is quite the cosmic mic drop.

CHAPTER 5: THE ANATOMY OF THE BLESSING: THE FIVE PILLARS

Reflecting back on those first few pages of Scripture, that wondrous genesis of it all, you stumble upon a cosmic conversation that sets the stage for everything else: "Let us make mankind in our image, in our likeness..." (Genesis 1:26). Now, I can't help but imagine that moment as the Most High rolls out His divine blueprint, looks to the Son and the Spirit, and they nod, like master craftsmen about to create their magnum opus. Yet, it's not with marble or bronze, but with dust and breath that they're sculpting—fashioning us, you and me, with features inherited from the Divine.

And as if this initial act of creation wasn't enough to leave us awestruck, we then hear the call, "Be fruitful and multiply; fill the earth and subdue it" (Genesis 1:28). My friends, this isn't just a mantra for propagation; it's the inaugural address to humanity outlining our purpose and place in this grand narrative. It's like we've all been handed generational gold tickets to adventure in God's kaleidoscopic kingdom. But what does it truly mean to live in the resemblance of our Maker and to flourish in this commission? Well, buckle up, because that's where the Five Pillars of The Blessing come into play, guiding us through the garden gates and into the nitty-gritty of our God-given roles on this big blue marble.

Genesis 1:28 KJV: "And God blessed them, and God said unto them, Be fruitful, and multiply, and replenish the earth, and subdue it: and have dominion over the fish of the sea, and over the fowl of the air, and over every living thing that moveth upon the earth." Now isn't that just like getting the heavenly keys to the family car? He's trusting us with His creation, giving us both the freedom and the responsibility to journey through life, to explore this "terra incognita" with love, stewardship, and a sense of wonder.

Oh, the exhilarating yet terrifying liberty of holding those keys! It reminds me of my first solo drive in my mom's old station wagon —the windows down, the uncertainties of the road up ahead, and my hands gripping the wheel like I was holding onto the edges of a way too literal life raft. There's a giddiness in knowing you could go anywhere, coupled with the sobering realization that maybe you should have paid a bit more attention during those driver's ed classes. That's how it can feel when we consider our purpose in this world: endless possibility tinged with a whisper of trepidation. But here's the kicker, folks—we aren't tossed the keys without a roadmap.

You know, understanding The Blessing is a bit like checking out a map before hitting the open road. It's God's trusty GPS for life's journey, complete with turn-by-turn directions to lead us with intention and love. Think of the Five Pillars as our signposts, the markers that helped Adam chart his life's adventure—and they're still helping us today. Just as Adam and Eve were handed the task of tending to creation, we've got our own slice of Eden to look after, all within the framework of these life-giving Pillars. Together, they're our guide to not just living, but flourishing in this wild, wonderful world we've been blessed to call home.

1. **Be Fruitful** - This is not just about producing offspring or tending to an orchard until it bursts with produce, though those are splendid things indeed. To 'be fruitful' is

to yield results that are ripe with significance and purpose—spiritual apples, if you will—that bear the sweet flavor of our partnership with the Creator. As the psalmist sings in Psalm 1:3, to be like a tree planted by streams of water, yielding fruit in due season. It's a reminder that our actions have the power to impact others and bring glory to God.

2. **Multiply** - Now here's where things get interesting. Multiplication isn't solely for bunnies and bank accounts—though who would turn down some extra multiplication in those areas? Biblically, to 'multiply' is to increase in numerous aspects; it's about heritage and influence, sprinkling seeds of faith and watching them grow far beyond our individual plots of land. In Deuteronomy 7:13, we're reminded that our love for Him leads to blessing, spurring a growth that spills over cups and runs down tables. To multiply, oh my friends, is an endeavor that tickles the soul and expands the pockets of the universe with love and laughter. The Hebrew word for multiply, *rabah*, is a delightful call to action, beckoning us to enlarge, to make great, increase.

3. **Replenish** - This jewel in the blessing crown invites us to refill and restore, not just use up resources like a kid in a candy shop with a five-dollar bill. Replenishing is about sustainable spiritual practices, pouring into others from a place of wholeness as God continuously refills your cup. In Isaiah 58:11, the Lord promises to guide you continually, providing even in dry deserts. Doesn't that just quench your spiritual thirst? Adam was to be the conduit through whom heaven would replenish the earth. It's profound, isn't it? Like Adam, we're called to be God's hands and feet, His direct line for divine deliveries of rejuvenation. We're here to pass on, or 'sub-let' if you will, bits of heaven unto this world with the same tender care one might use to transplant seedlings. Whether it's sharing wisdom with a neighbor or planting trees for future generations to enjoy the shade, our lives

echo the grand purpose that was set in the Garden. Every act of love, every shared insight is a sprinkle of that heavenly water, promising to turn deserts into orchards over time.

4. **Subdue** - Now, 'subdue' might bring to mind a wrestling match, but it's really about bringing order to chaos, like the conductor of a breathtaking symphony—or let's say, orchestrating a family dinner where no food gets thrown. When life gets a tad unruly, remember Mark 4:39 where Jesus calms the sea. He's our role model for quelling life's tempests and teaching those boisterous waves (and sometimes children) to simmer down. Isn't it something, how a word from Jesus could hush the howling winds and make waves lie down like obedient pups? Sure puts my meek shushes to a rowdy room to shame. But that's just it—when Jesus spoke to that storm, He was showing us a snapshot of what blessing really looks like. It's this divine authority, an assurance that when He tells us we can speak to mountains, hey, those mountains better get ready to take a swim. Now, 'subdue' doesn't mean you throw your weight around like a bouncer at heaven's VIP door. No, it's about mastery, gentle but firm, like how you'd whisper a fervent prayer against a tornado of troubles, knowing your whispered words carry the weight of Heavenly coin. It's Jesus' way of reminding us to stand firm, assert our blessed heritage, and command the chaos to take a back seat because, friends, He's already secured our victory.

5. **Have Dominion** - And then we talk dominion. Not a heavy-handed rule, but rather, caring with authority—like a benevolent king or maybe a master gardener who tends every leaf and bloom with love. Jesus is our primer here, demonstrating in John 13:3-5 that having all authority means we get down and wash some feet. It's that royal call to stewardship, where true power is shown through service. So let's continue this journey of faith with an open heart and a humble spirit, knowing that our ultimate goal is to follow in the footsteps of Jesus. We can learn from His example

of using our authority not for selfish gain, but for the betterment of others.

Reflecting on the richness of The Blessing, it's like unwrapping a gift that keeps on giving. It's not just about receiving; it's about stepping into a kind of spiritual inheritance that morphs our trials into triumphs. Like that little glow worm of hope that winks at you in the darkest tunnel—The Blessing is a steadfast beacon of God's promise. When we're told we have dominion, it's not a power trip ticket; it's a nudge to nurture, to serve, to love with a capital 'L'. To be blessed is to have an invisible crown that only shines when we bow to lift another. So let's wear that crown, shall we? And let's wear it with the kind of quiet confidence that speaks volumes without shouting, whispering to the world that, indeed, we are beloved children of an extravagantly loving God.

The Church, my friends, is yearning for those with their spiritual boots laced tight, who meander the earth with the blessings tightly knit into the fabric of their souls. We've seen the elaborate rituals, the solemn faces in Sunday pews, but what ignites the heavens is the unscripted dance of the true sons and daughters of God. Those who don't just carry blessings like hidden treasures but fling them wide for the world to catch.

You see, when all five pillars—Fruitful, Multiply, Replenish, Subdue, and Dominion—are not just words we echo but are the very ground we tread upon, that's when the Kingdom unfolds around us, almost as if the air itself shimmers with possibility. It's not about thumping a Bible upon a pulpit, but living out scripture on the dusty roads of life. Can you feel it? It's in the way we reach for the forgotten, how we love the unlovely, and in those honest moments when we're more shepherd than king.

So, here's a toast—to the passersby who become pilgrims, to the listeners who become storytellers, to the blessed who become blessings. It's time to declare the goodness of the Kingdom, not just in hushed prayers but in joyous proclamations, living each day as a display of those five profound pillars.

CHAPTER 6: SPIRIT-LED LIVING: THE CRUCIAL KEY TO UNLOCKING TRUE ABUNDANCE

You know, I've often thought about what it means to live a life led by the Spirit. Candidly speaking, it wasn't always clear to me—it's not like you get a thundering voice from the heavens with step-by-step instructions (though, how easy would that be?). It's more like finding your rhythm in a dance, a dance where the steps are not so much learned as they are revealed, one by one, through the quiet nudges that echo in the chambers of your soul.

I remember one brisk autumn morning, the kind where the air is crisp enough to make you feel alive and your breath fogs in front of you like a cloud of mystery. I felt a tug, a subtle inkling to forgo my well-laid plans and head down to the river's edge. No reason, really—just a sense that I needed to be by the water. Sitting there, the ripples spoke in hushed tones of a love so pervasive that it's woven into the very threads of creation. It dawned on me; this is what spirit-led living must be—attuning our spiritual senses to the gentle rhythm of God's soft whispers, aligning our hearts to beat with His.

And in those moments of quietude by the water's edge, I can't help but think of Ezekiel—standing by the river Chebar when the heavens opened and he saw visions of God. The Spirit led him there, not by his own compass but by divine inclination. It's a vibrant reminder that Spirit-led living isn't just about us tuning in to God; it's about becoming finely attuned instruments in His orchestra, playing out a melody crafted before time.

You see, Spirit-led living is to walk the path of Jesus, who, full of the Holy Spirit, retreated into the wilderness. It wasn't His idea of a getaway; it was the Spirit's leading that brought Him face to face with temptations, with hunger, with the rawness of life. But it was also the Spirit that fortified Him, that turned solitude into solace, strengthening His resolve for the ministry that lay ahead.

Have you ever had one of those days where every red light seems to have it out for you, every coffee pot is determined to pour its bitterness into your cup, and every shoelace is on a personal mission to trip you up? And in the middle of that dance with Murphy's Law, there's this still, small voice inviting you to look beyond the surface commotion. That's the whisper of Spirit-led living, transforming everyday mishaps into a symphony of footsteps guided by grace.

In a way, these moments are like spiritual checkpoints, little nudges reminding us to pause and see the bigger picture. When we embrace these prompts from the Spirit, we're signing up for an adventure that's far more about the journey than the destination. There's a richness in letting go of our meticulously drawn maps and discovering that, maybe, we don't need a destination when we're already where we need to be—in the presence of the Divine, who turns our mess into a message, our tests into testimonies.

Let's not forget, living a life led by the Spirit isn't synonymous with an easy life. It is, however, lined with the beauty of becoming; becoming more patient, more loving, more resilient. So yes, spirit-led living might take you through the wilderness, and you might get acquainted with a few lions on the way (hopefully not the Daniel-type!), but it's the same path that leads to mountains with views too magnificent for words. Now, isn't that a journey worth taking?

Have you ever gone for a stroll in the crisp morning air, where each step on the dew-sprinkled grass feels like a new conversation with the Earth? There's a sense of companionship as your feet keep rhythm with nature's pulse. It's in this same sacred cadence Adam must've walked with God—unhurried and full of anticipation for each day's fresh dialogues. It's that daily communion, where the whispers of dawn promise more than just the sun's warm embrace, that offers a glimpse into what it means to walk with the Divine.

And then there's Enoch, who 'walked with God; then he was no more, because God took him away.' (Genesis 5:22). This always makes me chuckle and think, "Well, that escalated quickly!" But isn't it just like life? One minute you're taking a leisurely stroll with your Creator, and the next thing you know, you're embarking on an eternal adventure. And Noah, oh dear Noah—his strolls led him into stormy seas but with the assurance that the deluge could never wash away the blessing of his walk with God.

The Spirit-led life, my friends, is inherently a blessed life. It's that recognition that, come storms or drought, we are covered by such blessings that turn our walk into a divinely choreographed dance. As we saunter through the subsequent chapters, let's unpack the potent blessings intertwined with the faithful strides of Noah and Abraham. These patriarchs were more than mere characters in an ancient narrative; they were trailblazers whose steps drew the blueprint of a life enveloped in God's favor. So, lace up your spiritual boots—we're about to embark on a walk through their lives that will reveal the secrets of walking with God, each step sprinkled with blessings and life-altering lessons.

CHAPTER 7: NOAH: SAVED BY GRACE, EMPOWERED BY THE BLESSING.

If there was ever a time when the grace of God was vividly portrayed in a person's life, it was in the story of Noah. This man found himself building an ark amidst unrelenting mockery - talk about sticking to a divine blueprint when everyone else is using the world's sketchpad! Noah's life seemed to follow the plot of a strange movie, where the protagonist hears a voice that others don't and acts on a faith that's invisible to the naked eye.

I remember this one time I tried building a treehouse as a kid in our backyard. Equipped with the best intentions but the poorest of carpentry skills, I hammered away, and well, let's just say it didn't quite end up as the sanctuary I had envisioned. The first gust of wind and that treehouse swayed like it was in a hula hoop competition. But not our man Noah; his ark didn't just sway —it floated triumphantly over the waves that wiped the slate of creation clean.

Can we take a moment to appreciate that? Amidst torrents of rain and surging floodwaters that likely turned his world into an endless sea, Noah's ark stood as a testament to being 'saved by grace'. But it wasn't just the physical preservation; it was the promise of a reset, the empowerment of a blessing that gave humanity a fresh start. Indeed, the tale of Noah is a reminder that when the world around us seems to dissolve into chaos, the blessings we gather through walking with God are our lifeboats, crafted not from gopher wood, but from promises that withstand the test of time and tempest.

So as we waddle through the puddles of our everyday storms, let's carry with us the buoyancy of Noah's faith. It's the kind of unwavering trust that turns a deluge into a baptismal pool, where we emerge not just surviving, but thriving – buoyed by grace, empowered by blessing, and ready to sail into our next chapter with a story that would make even the fiercest storm pause and say, "That's some kind of faith."

Genesis 6:8, what a gem of a verse! It's like finding that last piece of chocolate in a forgotten Easter basket. Here we have our guy Noah, living in an age where the hit reality show might as well have been called 'When Humankind Goes Wild.' Virtue seemed as rare as a payphone in today's world. Yet, in all that mess, Noah was like that one clean shirt in a pile of laundry – he stood out.

But when the Good Book says, "Noah found grace in the eyes of the LORD," what's it really whispering to us through the ages? It's like this; imagine you're in a crowded room, feeling a tad invisible, and someone who truly matters spots you from across the chaos. Their eyes light up. That's grace—a divine spotlight that says, "I see you. You matter." This isn't just a pat on the back for being a good egg. Nope, it's unearned, like stumbling upon a treasure while digging for potatoes. Grace is underserved favor; it's God's way of giving us a thumbs-up, telling us we've got a role in this sprawling epic of creation, even when the script seems to have gone awry. It's God calling an audible in the playbook for humanity.

Grace is a bit like an umbrella in a rainstorm—it doesn't stop the downpour, but it sure does keep you dry. Noah was hunkered down in that ark, not just shielded by the Almighty's grace but also appointed to reboot humanity. And there's something profoundly beautiful about stepping out of that ark, a world washed clean, yet dauntingly empty. Like stepping out from Grandma's cozy kitchen into the big wide world, you realize the hand that guided you through the storm wants you to dance in the aftermath and plant new gardens.

But here's the rub—freedom is more than just breaking chains. It's the courage to dream on open plains. The blessing, that's the muscle, the how-to of making Eden blossom in places that only knew wilderness. I've seen it, the way those freed from the yoke stumbled, not because their spirits weren't willing, but hands that should plant and build were left empty. And aren't it just the way, when folks have just tasted freedom, trouble comes knocking, trying to steal the very dream that got them through those nights.

In my own walk, I've seen the shadows of those long-gone shackles. But, brothers and sisters, we aren't called to be shadowboxers; we're called to be architects of light. We are the body of Christ, and it's high time we harmonize our grace-filled melodies with the rhythm of the blessing. Whether you hail from the corners of Harlem or the banks of the Mississippi, it's our collective hands that will heal, build, and gather, sowing seeds not just for survival, but for a legacy.

So, what comes after the floodwaters recede and the doves of peace have done their flyby with a fresh olive branch? Well, it's that first squelch of mud beneath your boots, isn't it? It's the promise that life—messy, glorious life—springs anew. I remember planting my first post-deluge garden, fingers caked with earth, sweat mixing with leftover rain. Seeds tucked into their earthen beds like children whispered away with a prayer and a bedtime story. And, oh, the waiting! The soul's whispered plea to the unseen. But then, the green shoots broke through, and my heart did a 2-step right there in the dirt.

Now, lest you think it's all daisies and sunshine, let's be real— blessings in the form of muddy gardens come with backaches and blisters. But think of it this way: the Lord's favor, the blessings we share, they're not just sprinkles on a sundae or the cherry on top. Nope, they are the rich soil, the compost that turns yesterday's rot into today's nourishment. And when those blessings start flowing, it's not just a trickle—it's a river that swells its banks to infuse those barren places with life aplenty.

It's almost comical, is it not? How a body, drenched to the bone, barren lands within sight, can stand firm and claim that patch of mud as holy? But that's the crux of it. With blessings comes the charge to transform, to steward this spinning globe of green and blue. Friends, we are gardeners of Eden reborn, with a calling to cultivate beauty from the chaos, joy from the jagged spaces life throws our way.

And like Noah, who, amidst the dewy freshness post-deluge, planted a vineyard as an act of hope and celebration, we too are summoned to bear fruit in abundance. We do so not for glory of our own, but as a sweet offering to the Father who has blessed us richly. It's a bit like making wine, isn't it? The process is as soul-fulfilling as it is soul-fraying—crushing those grapes underfoot, rejoicing in the laughter that echoes through the vines, and yes, even savoring the tang of fermentation's bite. There's a divine alchemy in turning life's water into wine, and we partake in this mystery with every small act of love, every hardship turned testimony. We cultivate our inner vineyards, prune the unruly vines, and trust in the Lord of the Harvest for the increase—knowing that the most profound growth often comes from the deepest roots. So let us then, with sleeves rolled up and hearts wide open, tend to our plots with the diligence of those who know the weight and the wonder of blessings. Let us grow, let us love, and let us lift our brimming cups to the sky—a toast to the One whose rains and sunshine coax the very best from the soil of our souls.

CHAPTER 8: ABRAM: FROM UR TO CANAAN

Dear friends, let us gather and tread into the dust-laden tales of old, where the whispers of history and the divine intertwine in an intricate dance. Picture Abram, before the weight of an extra "h" in his name, dwelling cozily in the land of Ur—a place vividly named after flames. It's a bit like living on the edge of desire itself, isn't it? Ur, a place crackling with ambition, burning with the heat of human wants and pride.

But then, he is called to Canaan, which means the Lowland—aptly named for its posture of humility against the backdrop of life's grandeur. To step into the foothold of blessings, to really wear the garment of God's promises like a well-fitting suit, Abram had to uproot from the familiar ash of Ur to the fertile humility of Canaan.

Abram's journey, then, is not merely a physical relocation—it is the pilgrimage of the soul seeking the soft cadence of the Spirit. Imagine the uproar in Ur, the clang and clash of city life, where whispers of eternity are drowned in the market's raucous. There's little room for the divine nudge amidst the jostle of ambitions and the auctioneer's relentless call.

To hear God, Abram had to embrace the stillness of Canaan, a place where silence speaks louder than the cacophony of progress. Have you ever noticed how it's in the quiet that our inner ears adjust to the frequency of the divine? You see, sometimes, like Abram, we're nudged to leave behind our personal 'Urs'—to seek out our

Lowland that's ripe for revelation. Abram, in the quietude, even a whisper became a clarion call, and his heart learned to listen—a skill as precious as it is rare.

And isn't it the same for us? To inherit the spirit-led life, to truly flourish in the generational blessings, we must often untangle ourselves from the very desires that once kept us warm at night. To build a legacy, much like Abram, we must step beyond the comfort zones, beyond the flicker of our own flame—and off the ledge into the unknown.

To allow ourselves to be led by the Spirit rather than our own burning longings, to flow in the promise of abundance—we move, just as Abram moved, from the fires of Ur to the humbled earth of Canaan. It's never easy, dear ones, leaving behind the familiar sounds and scents of home. But in the thick of our personal Edens, we see a truth as clear as day: Humility is the key, the golden key that turns the lock to a life worn beautifully, adorned with the jewels of Spirit-led living.

Abram's first steps in Canaan were not without trepidation; it was a canvas unhewn, a tapestry unwoven. Can you imagine the surging mix of apprehension and hope, much like when we step out in faith—not quite knowing if we're diving into boundless grace or an abyss? There, amidst the untamed sheaves of Canaan, the Divine promise was spread like a feast for the faithful. And still, Abram built altars—not to claim victories or future successes —but as humble stone memos, reminders to himself of the One who calls us forth from the womb of comfort.

Just the other day, I found myself at a crossroads, quite literally, standing at the corner of 'What If' Avenue and 'I Trust You' Street. The funny thing is, crossroads don't come with maps; it's the silent nudges, the soft murmurings unfelt by calloused ambition, that point the way. In Canaan, Abram didn't find a flickering neon sign but received the slow drip of assurance, the kind that deepens roots rather than misplacing them like tumbleweeds. It's the kind of deep knowing that grounds us, reminding us that our encounters with the sacred are less about the loud and monumental and more about the soft, steady chorus of creation that hums if we just take the time to listen.

Abram's first steps in Canaan were not those of a conqueror or a self-proclaimed chosen one. They were the humble steps of a faithful servant, trusting in the guidance and provision of Adonai. And so it is with us, as we journey through our own spiritual landscapes. We must follow in Abram's footsteps, building altars along the way to remind ourselves that it is not our own strength or merit that carries us forward, but the grace and love of a higher power.

We must embrace humility and persevere through challenges with eternal optimism, knowing that even in the darkest moments, there is always hope and growth to be found. We are called to walk in Abram's footsteps, trusting in the journey and finding strength in humility. Continue on this path, with open hearts and a spirit of perseverance, knowing that we are not alone but always guided by a loving higher power.

Oh, the winding paths of humility! It has its thorns, its unexpected turns, but it's the gateway to living a life of blessing. Imagine, if you will, Abram standing at a crossroad with Lot, with the vastness of Canaan stretching out in every direction. Heaven had whispered promises into Abram's very soul, yet here he stood, offering Lot the first pick. (Genesis 13:5-11)

Now, to the onlooker, it might've seemed like Abram had lost his marbles, giving up his divine right so freely. But see, Abram had kneeled at the altar of humility and found strength there— a quiet might that looked beyond the immediate, perceiving the everlasting tapestry being woven by the Most High. In a moment of potential strife, humility was Abram's compass, guiding him towards peace.

Doesn't it just tickle your ribs to think about Lot choosing Sodom? Like a moth to a flame, he darts back to what Abram had left—

a life buzzing with noise and chaos, mirroring his own unsettled spirit.

Even later, when Lot found himself in dire straits, who rides out like a valiant, yet humble, knight? Abram—yes, our humble hero, who knew that true strength isn't about grandstanding, but about standing grandly when the moment demands. Thus, the lion of humility roared, not in pride, but in righteous protection backed by the legions of heaven.

Let's not forget, that humility isn't about bowing low to the ground; it's about standing tall in spirit, ready to be a conduit of blessings. For by wearing humility like a mantle, you become not only the blessed but the very blessing itself, a vessel of concealed strength ready to pour out like an endless river when the world is parched for just a drop of kindness.

Lot stood with Abram, gazing out at the vastness of Canaan stretched before them. It was a land promised to Abram by God Himself, a testament to His faithfulness and love. Yet here he was, offering Lot the first choice in this new land. To an outsider, it may have seemed like Abram was foolishly giving up his divine right. But in truth, he was yielding to the greater power of humility and showing Lot that true strength lies not in possessions or position, but in a humble heart. And with that act, Abram's legacy as a great leader and man of God was cemented for all generations to come.

At times, it may seem difficult to maintain humility when facing challenges or making sacrifices. But through Abram's example, we are reminded that humility is not weakness, but rather a source of strength and grace. It allows us to see beyond our own desires and needs, and instead focus on the well-being of others and the greater good. By embracing humility, we can become vessels for blessings, channels for love and kindness in a world that often lacks these qualities. And in doing so, we continue the legacy of great leaders like Abram, who showed us that true strength lies in the power of humility.

CHAPTER 9: FROM ABRAM TO ABRAHAM: THE FATHER OF MANY NATIONS

There's something deeply profound about the way God flips the script in our lives, just when we think we've got the storyline all figured out. Picture it: Abram, settled into his golden years, probably anticipating a quiet life, gets the divine equivalent of a plot twist. It's like God Himself sat down, shuffled the deck of destiny, and dealt out a hand no one saw coming.

Abram, who had become something of an expert in the fine art of standing firm in faith—whether before kings or kin—didn't realize that he was just in the opening chapters of his journey. Heaven was set on a narrative of multiplication that would leave Abram's name forever etched in the annals of spiritual heritage, but there was a snag in the script: It wasn't Abram who was destined to father nations; it was Abraham.

Now, this might sound like a mere name change, but it's as significant as trading your bicycle for a spaceship. In Genesis 17, when God announces the name change, He's not just giving Abram a spiritual rebranding. He's signaling a shift to an identity so vast and so full of potential that it takes divine intervention to step into it. And here's the kicker: Abram had been leaning on his old buddy, understanding, crafting solutions with Sarai, that well, let's say, were more human-sized. We've all been there, haven't we? Making sense of things with our limited blueprints and ending up with ish-mess—Oops, I mean Ishmaels.

The joyous punchline comes when God rewrites Abram's job description from childless nomad to progenitor of a multitude. And all poor Abram had to do was to let go of his handy-dandy understanding, trust in a plan he couldn't map out, and step into a new pair of sandals fit for a father of faith. Decades might seem like an awfully long time to wait for a childhood dream to come true, but then again, divine timing has a penchant for dramatic entrances—just ask Abraham as he cradled Isaac.

So, here's a toast to life's spiritual migrations—from Abram to Abraham. May our own journeys be lined with the triumphant chuckles of having our understanding gently unraveled by a God who dreams infinitely bigger than we do.

The beauty of this story lies not only in the dramatic shift from Abram to Abraham, but also in the fact that God chose to use a flawed and imperfect human being as His vessel. It serves as a reminder that our struggles and doubts do not disqualify us from fulfilling our purpose in life.

Proverbs 4:5 does an elegant dance, urging us to get wisdom, but oh, to also grab hold of understanding with all we've got. And I can't help but agree – understanding isn't the villain of our story; it's the sidekick that sometimes gets a bit too cheeky for its breeches. I mean, who can blame it? We're wired to yearn for the 'why' and the 'how'.

But there lies the rub, just as it did for our dear Abram. We're made in God's image, yes, and that's an honor that could puff up any chest with pride. Yet here's the divine whisper in the rustling leaves of our lives – don't lean too hard on that self-crafted crutch of personal insight. It's like trying to listen to a symphony with cotton buds stuck in your ears; you miss the fullness of the Heavenly melody.

Abram, bless his heart, figured this out the curve that understanding might just be the hand holding yours, not the feet walking the path. God's blueprint for him was a splash of divine genius – from a man scraping the skies with his hopes to the father of nations. Now, if we can only trust in the Divine's plan, even when our understanding seems to be squinting at a foggy road sign, well, we might just find ourselves laughing at the stars, Abraham-style.

CHAPTER 10: THE ABRAHAMIC BLESSING

You might say a blessing is a bit like that unexpected care package from a loved one—that box of goodness that lands on your doorstep when you need it most. It's a divine favor, a sprinkle of heaven's own spices into the stew of our everyday lives. A blessing doesn't just add flavor, though. Oh no, it transforms the mundane into something...worthy of a table set before kings.

In the design of our faith, to bestow a blessing is to weave golden threads of grace, hope, and destiny into the fabric of another soul. It's as though God Himself passes by, humming a tune of prosperity and peace that settles in around the shoulders like a well-worn shawl. Sometimes, it feels tangible, like the warm sunbeam that dances across your face on a chilly morning, softly whispering, "I see you. I've got you."

But get this—sometimes the blessing is wrapped up in a disguise of adversity. It knocks on our door, and we're tempted to say, "You've got the wrong address, buddy!" We may not recognize it immediately, but in the sacred hush after our grumbling ceases, we begin to understand that each challenge carves out space for growth, leaving a little more room for joy, strength, and that tenacious thing called resilience.

So when we speak of Abraham and the blessings he scurried after, remember, it's not just about acquiring that prime real estate in the sky. It's the sacred exchange between the Divine and the devoted—the promise of a legacy as numerous and brilliant as the stars above. And that, dear friends, is something we can tuck into our pockets as we journey through our own zigzagging paths, don't you think?

Oh, the blessing to Abraham, you ask? That was the lifeline on his spiritual GPS, a compass that didn't just point north, but upwards and into the unseen. Consider the stars that shimmer like a net full of fireflies caught by a curious child—that's the magnitude of the promise Abraham clung to. The blessing didn't just sprinkle success on Abraham's path; it injected his very steps with purpose, courage, and a smidge of divine chutzpah.

Every ripple of his faithfulness, every echo of his laughter echoing through his tent, they were the sound waves of heaven cheering him on. For Abraham, the blessings were more than a badge of honor—they were the reassurance that the Creator of galaxies and the counter of hairs on our heads wasn't just making idle chit-chat when He handed out promises. That blessing, my friends, stitched together the tapestry of his legacy with threads of trust that were tested, alright, but as unbreakable as, well, divine guarantees can get. And yes, even amidst the laughable idea of parenting a nation at a ripe old age—because, let's be honest, that's a knee-slapper— those blessings whispered the sweet, sacred mantra: "I am with you; this is for you."

So, did the blessing matter to old Abe and his journey to success? As much as caffeine matters to a Monday morning—that's a resounding yes coated in a whole lot of holy moly! So, dear friends, let's remember the importance of blessings in our own lives and allow them to propel us forward on our faith journey. Let's hold onto them as tightly as we hold onto each other in times of trouble. Because just like Abraham, we too have been blessed with purpose, courage, and a divine chutzpah to persevere through any challenges that come our way. And that, my friends, is a promise we can hold onto with unwavering faith and hope. So let's keep on keeping on, knowing that the Creator of all things has blessed us and is with us every step of the way.

As we navigate life's challenges and chase our dreams, may we remember the story of Abraham and how his faith was strengthened by the blessings he received from God. Let's also reflect on our own blessings and how they have shaped us into the unique individuals we are today. And let's not forget to share those blessings with others, spreading hope and encouragement wherever we go.

Remember, dear readers, that no matter what obstacles we face or doubts we may have, we are blessed by a loving and faithful God who is always with us. We must hold onto our blessings, embrace our faith journey, and trust in the unbreakable guarantees of divine grace and guidance. The journey may not always be easy, but we can have confidence in knowing that we are never alone on this path. As Abraham's story reminds us, blessings are a reminder of God's unwavering love and faithfulness towards us, even in the midst of difficult times. So let's keep pushing forward, holding onto our blessings and trusting in God's plan for our lives.

There is no limit to what we can achieve with faith and blessings on our side! Keep shining bright, dear friends, as you walk hand in hand with the One who lightens your our path. It is ok to chuckle a little when you trip over life's unexpected pebbles – we're all awkwardly dancing through life's rhythm, sometimes stepping on our own toes. I've done it plenty, believe me. And, oh, how the heavens must have laughed along with me! Through these moments, I've seen glimmers of joy – the kind that comes from not taking ourselves too seriously and the warm, hearty laughter shared with fellow journeyers.

Let's wrap up this chapter with a quiet moment of gratitude, a little prayer whispered or shouted, whatever suits your heart best today. Think of it as a cosmic 'thank you note' for the wild, wondrous journey so far and for the companionship of the One who promises to walk beside us into whatever chapters lie ahead.

Here's to the next steps, the next laughs, and the next leaps of faith. May we jump with both feet, hearts full and eyes open to the starlit possibilities that await us. Because, at the end of the day, we're all blessed stargazers, aren't we? We're searching the skies, not just for guidance, but also for the beauty woven into our lives' stories.

I can't wait to see where our travels take us next. But for now, breathe deeply, step confidently, and remember – the journey itself is the destination, and what a magnificent journey it is.

CHAPTER 11: THE BLESSING OF CHRIST: THE FATHER'S APPROVAL

Have you ever seen a child's face light up under the beaming pride of their parents? There's this unmistakable glow, kind of like when the first rays of dawn grace the sky—hopeful and warm. It's this approval we often yearn for, a sign that we're on the right track. Now, I've stumbled more times than I'd like to admit, hoping for that celestial pat on the back. But here's the thing: In Christ's blessing, we find the ultimate Father's approval. It's the nod of 'You're doing just fine, kid' from the heavens.

One afternoon, nestled on my favorite park bench that's seen better days (we're both a bit weathered), I mused over my need for approval. That's when it hit me—like that time I forgot the tent stakes on a camping trip and the tent flew off—it's not about earning His approval. We already have it!

In this chapter, let's unpack the treasure trove of acceptance we've inherited. Like a cozy blanket on a chilly evening, the Father's approval wraps around us, offering comfort as we navigate life's quirks and quandaries. It's in the serene stillness we sometimes sense on a chaotic Monday, or in the vigor we feel when we're about to give up but suddenly find ourselves pressing on. So come along—grab your metaphorical spade as we dig for the gold of divine acceptance, even if you're like me and sometimes forget where you put your actual gardening tools (I swear they have legs). Here's to discovery and the ever-present, loving nod from above.

Oh, the journey of faith—picture it as a winding trail, not too different from my last misadventure of a hike where I was sure I'd conquered the path, only to find I'd circled back to where I started (Who put that tree there last time?). On this trek, we might get the sense that our place at the table with Christ is something akin to a spiritual game of musical chairs, constantly in flux, based on our latest blunders or triumphs.

But, here's a comforting thought, one that found me as I sat nursing a bruised knee, quite literally, after a pothole encounter: Christ's blessing and acceptance aren't fickle prizes to be won; they're foundational. These aren't earned through a spiritual résumé or lost in a moment of waywardness. No, my friends, they're as consistent as my mom's Sunday pot roast—always there, always hearty, ready to nourish.

In that very real tumble, with humility kissing my ego, I realized acceptance isn't about perfect alignment with a set of divine expectations. It's present in each dust-off, each new start. The blessing lies not in flawless living but in being fully known, and loved, dirt smudges and all. Christ's acceptance is an invitation to rest in grace as surely as my old Siberian Husky, Ghost , flops down for a nap—unconcerned, secure.

Reflecting on the importance of the Father's approval pulls me back to childhood memories of learning to ride a bike—those wobbly moments when the steadying hand at the back was my only assurance I wouldn't topple over. It left me pondering, why is this paternal nod, this celestial thumbs-up, so fundamental in the grand cosmic ballet?

See, the Father's approval is that quiet whisper reminding us that we're part of a larger story, a grand masterpiece masterfully constructed of divine purpose. It's the reassuring baseline in the symphony of our existence, always playing beneath the sounds of our daily hustle. In those tender moments when self-doubt casts its shadow, the importance of His thumbs-up is clearer than the time my spectacles finally were after a much-delayed cleaning. It's a validation of our inherent worth, an affirmation that we're more than our flaws, more enduring than our ephemeral successes and failures.

In the grand scheme of things, it resonates with the truth that our value doesn't ebb and flow with the tides of human judgement or heavenly scorekeeping. The Father's approval matters not because it's a ticket to some exclusive club, but because it's an anchor in the turbulent seas, an enduring embrace that whispers, "You are loved, you are seen, just as you are." And just like my dear dog Ghost, who never questioned his place by the fireside, we're invited to bask in the warmth of this eternal assurance, without fear of the cold.

In my book, "The Seed of Righteousness," I delve deeper into this dance of divine approval—a tango of transcendence that teaches us the rhythmic steps of walking in the approbation of the Father upon the Son, Jesus Christ. It's a spiritual soiree that many miss, choosing instead to sit listlessly on the sidelines. But dear friends, it's in this very dance that we discover the full suite of God's couture righteousness—a garment tailored to fit our souls. This blessing we speak of, it's no mere pat on the back; it's the undeniable evidence of us operating within the showroom of His righteousness.

And so, with the eagerness of a kid at Christmas, I encourage—nay, I implore you—to read and mull over my study guide. "The Seed of Righteousness" isn't just another name on your bookshelf; it's a key. A key that unlocks the shackles of religious routine and frees you to stride into the identity draped over you with the care of a master weaver. It's an identity that isn't just a tag we wear; it's the very genesis of all blessings. The blessing, my fellow journeyers, isn't the destination. It's the breathtaking view along the path of His promises. So, come along, take hold of this truth, and step out in the identity that's more than an endowment—it's the elixir of life itself.

CHAPTER 12: JOINT HEIRS WITH CHRIST

There's something both humbling and exhilarating about being a joint heir with Christ, isn't there? It's like winning the heavenly lottery—and not just because we got lucky, but because we were chosen by name. Now, wouldn't that warm the innermost parts of your heart? The truth is, praying "Our Father, who art in heaven" isn't meant to be a solo recital. It's a chorus, a harmony of hearts connected to Christ, our head. This unity—it's not an idea plucked from thin air; it's the spiritual WiFi that connects the body of believers.

Yes, friend, this is a truth we're called to live out loud, not just mumble under our breath. We advertise the kingdom of God not with flashy billboards but through our lives, lived as authentic ambassadors, emissaries of grace. When we speak, our words should be like hand-delivered letters from God Himself, perfumed with the fragrance of hope.

And here's the kicker: as much as we're seated in heavenly places —our feet might be tapping the earthly soil, yet, *He* is alive and kicking within us. The kingdom? It's not a distant realm. It's coded in our spiritual DNA. Christ in us—oh, the hope of glory! It's the hidden treasure the devil wishes we'd never find. But once we do, we become aliens to mediocrity, champions of the faith.

We're not who the enemy whispers we are. You see, our identity card isn't printed in the dungeons of deceit—it bears the seal of the King Himself. And activation? It's just a matter of belief—a simple, profound, life-altering belief. It's not about flaunting our spiritual resume; it's wearing the righteousness of Christ like a second skin. Beloved, join me in this divine dance of trust. For we are one with Jesus, and that, dear saints, is the most significant title we'll ever hold.

Ah, the grand tapestry of life, interwoven with threads of divine connection. Picture this, my friends: each family, a living, breathing showcase of the life we have in Christ. Imagine, if you will, our children's eyes lighting up as we live out the truth—we are co-heirs with Christ, not just in the sweet by-and-by, but right here, in the nitty-gritty of our daily walk. Our lives are meant to be billboards of belief, demonstrations of the divine, setting the stage for the generations to come. The enemy? Oh, he's quaking in his boots, terrified of the day we discover our royal lineage in the Kingdom.

Each day we're handed a chisel and a block of time, shaping the legacy we leave behind. We're artists and authors, sculpting a saga of faith that will echo through eternity. From glory to glory, faith to faith, we're leaving breadcrumbs of belief for our little ones to follow. So let's make it a feast of fidelity, a banquet of belief that fills them up and sends them soaring on the wings of legacy. That's our calling, beloved—to bind our hearts to the eternal pulse of the corporate Christ and show this world what Kingdom kinship is all about.

CHAPTER 13: THE CULTURE OF THE KINGDOM

Picture this: As members of the celestial consortium, we've got heaven in our veins and eternity etched into our very being. When you stop and ponder—that *right there* is the culture of the Kingdom; a divine pattern of living that isn't just a heavenly future, but a here-and-now reality.

You see, we're not just walking the earth, we're treading holy ground with each step, and the air we breathe? Well, it's laced with the aroma of promise. It's about every word whispered in prayer, every act of kindness that stems from the overflow of Christ within us, mirroring the culture of up above to all those we encounter. Every time we choose love over hate, peace over turmoil, and hope over despair, we're like those imperial British tea-drinkers, except we're serving up cups of salvation with a side of eternal hope!

So, let's turn the mundane into the hallowed, shall we? Let's drive on the left-hand side of the Kingdom road, joyously throwing God's promises like confetti over a world in dire need of celebration. And in our daily, sometimes messy, march of faith—may we be the unmistakable echo of a divine dialect, revealing just how wondrous life can be under God's glorious governance.

For as ambassadors of the Most High, we are charged with a holy mandate: to transplant the culture of heaven right into the soil of the earthly realm. Let's live out loud, brothers and sisters, as an invitation to those who've yet to taste the Kingdom; let's exemplify the language of love, the rhythm of redemption and the sovereignty of salvation. Let's expand this hallowed culture one saved soul, one changed life, one act of unmerited grace at a time —after all, we're not just telling the tale of Heaven, we're offering them the keys to the Kingdom!

The influence of Kingdom culture is like a hearty laugh that softens the sharp edges of a weary world—it's contagious, my friends! I remember this one time, I offered a smile and my seat to an elderly woman on the bus, and the next thing you know, it set off a chain reaction; people started chatting, sharing stories, and, oh, the goodness was spreading faster than that time my two-year-old niece found the glitter jar—the bus became a shimmering snapshot of Kingdom camaraderie. That's the thing about the culture of the Kingdom: it transforms spaces and hearts with the subtlety of sunrise, bathing the ordinary in extraordinary light.

When we deliberately carry the banner of the Most High into our everyday transactions, we're doing more than being good citizens—we're emulating Jesus with skin on. Whether doling out wholesome compliments like grandma's famous cookies or listening—really listening—to the cashier spill her heart along with our receipt, we're imparting the essence of the Kingdom. We live not just in moments of grand triumph but in those tiny, sacred acts of love that knit together the tapestry of eternity right here, on mortal turf. With chuckles in the face of adversity and boundless optimism, we prove that the impact of Kingdom culture isn't a far-off dream, but as tangible as the hand that wipes a tear, the whisper that nudges a dreamer, and the faith that leaps over mountains of doubt.

It's in the crumb-filled corners of our kitchens where sometimes the most profound Kingdom conversations take place. Over a cup of coffee that's maybe a little too strong (because who really measures anymore?), a friend poured out his worries just as freely as I poured another cup. We chuckled about our human tendency to make mountains out of molehills, but in that shared laughter, a peace that passes all understanding took up residence between us. It's the kind of peace that says, "you're not alone," knitting our spirits together in solidarity against life's storms.

I can't help but reflect on another time when that Kingdom kindness caught me by surprise. There was a young man in front of me at the supermarket—he was fumbling with his wallet, realizing that he couldn't cover his grocery bill. Stepping forward, I covered the difference; it wasn't much, but to him, it might as well have been a million bucks. His smile was a flash of light, like a beacon of hope that rewrote the narrative of his day, and honestly, mine too. Kingdom culture isn't heralded by the sound of trumpets; it's the gentle whisper of the Divine in these pockets of humanity, in the give and take of everyday grace. And every time we choose kindness, patience, and warmth, we plant seeds of His love, and truly, there's no telling how far that can grow. Now, if that isn't a reason to beam with optimism, I don't know what is!

So often, we imagine that to live a life of spiritual impact, we must embark on grand adventures or perform monumental tasks. But what I've discovered, in-between the extraordinary and the mundane, is that Kingdom culture thrives in the subtler frequencies of life. It's in the shared smiles with strangers, the hands held tight in prayer in hospital waiting rooms, and the extra scoop of ice cream you give to a child who's had a tough day. It's less about the loud declarations of faith and more about the quiet, steady pulse of love that courses through our daily acts of kindness.

To wrap up the tapestry of our musings, dear friends, let's remember that the essence of Kingdom culture isn't found in the toppling of giants but in the soft strength of love. It's a culture that blooms in the face of adversity, one that finds humor in the irony of our imperfections, and stands resilient in the quiet corners where hope whispers to the weary traveler, "Keep going."

As we turn the last page of this journey together, I leave you with this: may your days be punctuated with laughter that thunders through your darkest nights, and may your steps leave imprints of peace and joy in the soil of this Earth. And above all, keep your ears tuned to that gentle whisper, guiding you onward, always onward. Because you, dear sojourner, are a carrier of light, and wherever you go, you change the atmosphere.

Let's keep our hearts tender, our eyes soft, and our minds open. We may be but a flicker in the expanse of eternity, but what a bright and beautiful flicker we can be. Thanks for walking this path with me. Until our trails cross again, go in peace and live in grace. The Kingdom is within you, around you, and moving through you— today, and all the days to come. Amen, and amen.

Made in the USA
Columbia, SC
31 March 2024

33458928R00030